YOU Family and School

ROBERT A. CARTER, Ph.D.

Coordinator of Social Studies and Foreign Languages
Midland, Texas

EDITH McCALL

Reading Specialist
Hollister, Missouri

VERNON PRINZING, Ed. D.

Professor, Departments of Education and Geography
DePaul University, Chicago, Illinois

BENEFIC PRESS

WESTCHESTER, ILLINOIS

Library of Congress
Number 77-075865
ISBN 0-8175-5300-2

CONTENTS

This picture is you. You are part of this book. This picture is to help you remember this. When you see the picture on a page, remember what it means.

Data Bank

This sign is at the beginning of special places in the book. These places will tell you things about you, your family, or your school.

Investigation

This sign is at the beginning of other special places in the book. These pages will ask that you think about some of the things you have learned before.

TIME SKILLS

A page with this sign on it will help you learn about changes that take place from one time to another, such as from day to day or year to year.

CHART SKILLS

A page with this sign will have pictures, words, or numbers to tell you many things in a small space.

DIAGRAM SKILLS

This will be a page with a picture on it. The picture will show you a plan of how things work, how things are done, or what is happening inside of something.

GLOBE SKILLS

A page with this sign will help you learn about a globe, which is a large ball showing where land and water are on the earth.

MAP SKILLS

A page with this sign on it will help you learn some of the things a map can show, such as how to get from your house to school.

You are a girl or boy.

You are like other boys and girls.

You are not like them, too.

WORDS TO KNOW
different, 8
changed, 10
people, 15

You

Here you are.

You see girls.

You see boys.

You are like them in some ways.

You are not like them in some ways.

You are <u>different</u> in some ways.

8

Who Are You?

Who do you see?

What are they doing?

Who are you?

Are you a girl?

Are you a boy?

How old are you?

What can you do?

You Change

You were very little.

Now you are different.

You changed.

Now you are big.

Some times you are happy.

Some times you are not happy.

Some times you like to play.

Some times you just like to think.

How Do You Change?

Which one in the picture is like you?

How big were you as a baby?

How big are you now?

What can a baby do?

What can you do?

What will you do when you get bigger?

LOOKING AND THINKING

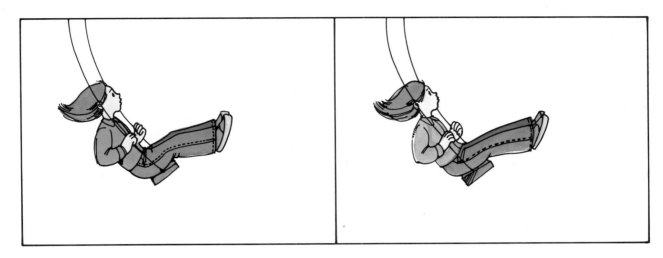

What changes do you see here?

What changes do you see here?

In which pictures did the boy or girl
stay the same?

13

You And Others

You are here.

You are at school.

You are with others.

14

You are at home.

You are with others.

You play with others.

You see other <u>people</u>.

You are like others.

You are different
from others.

How Are People Different?

How do these people look different?

How do they look the same?

How are you like other people?

How are you different?

To Talk About And To Do

Talk about children.

How are they the same and different?

Make a big picture to show the ways.

Why can you do more if all help?

Check What You Know

1. You were a baby.

   Now you are older.

   How did you change?

2. How do you change from day to day?

3. How are others like you?

Learning By Doing

Bring baby pictures to put up.

Tell who is in the pictures.

What would you do?

| GENERALIZING | **Checking Ideas** |

1. What can you tell about you?

2. How do you change?

3. What can you tell about others?

You are one in a family.

A family does things.

A family has happy days.

19

family, 20
remember, 28

Here Are Families

The baby has a mother.

The baby has a father.

The three are a family.

20

Some families have a
mother and father
and children.

Some families have a
mother and children.

Some families have a
father and children.

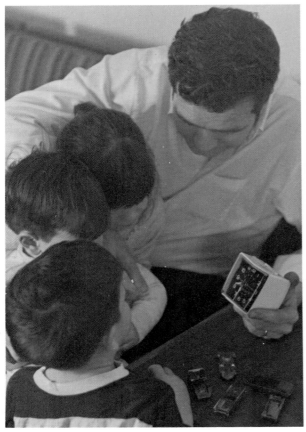

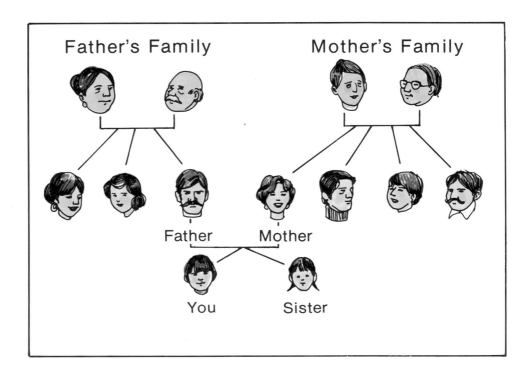

Father's Family   Mother's Family

Father   Mother

You   Sister

A Family Tree

A family tree tells about a family.

It shows all the people in a family.

Mother had a mother and father.

How many children were in her family?

Father had a family.

How many children were in his family?

What Is A Family?

Is this a family?

How can you tell?

What is a family?

Families Change

Here is a family.

The family is bigger.

Here is a family.

Then one is gone.

All families change.

They get big.

They get little.

Look at the picture.

It shows a change.

A family gets little.

Now there is a new family.

How Do Families Change?

This is a family.

How can it change?

How can the children change?

How may your family change?

Days Families Remember

The girl will think back to this day
for a long time.

She will remember it.

She is happy.

The family will remember this day.

They are happy, too.

Why will the girl remember this day?

People in families remember many days.

They remember them in different ways.

Many families remember this day.

How are the people in this family

remembering this day?

Mahalia Jackson

(1911-1972)

Mahalia Jackson was a little girl.

She liked to sing.

People asked her to sing for them.

Many people liked to hear her.

Singing was her work.

Did Mahalia like her work?

What work would you like to do?

Why?

What Days Does Your Family Remember?

Look at the first four pictures.

Do they help you think of days your family remembers?

What days?

Look at the other pictures.

Do they help you think of good days for your family?

What days?

31

Some things make a day to remember.

Look at the pictures.

What things show a day to remember?

Why?

To Talk About And To Do — GROUP ACTIVITY

Talk about things all of you can do
to make a day to remember.

All the children can help.

Why is it better when many help?

Check What You Know — EVALUATION

1. What does a family tree show?

2. In what ways do families change?

3. What can families do on days
that are good?

Learning By Doing — TIME SKILLS

Make a picture of your family
when you were three.

Make a picture of your family now.

How has your family changed?

VALUING	**Building Values**

The father's mother is coming to stay.

The family is changing.

What would you do?

GENERALIZING	**Checking Ideas**

1. What is a family?

2. How may a family change?

3. Why do you remember some
family days?

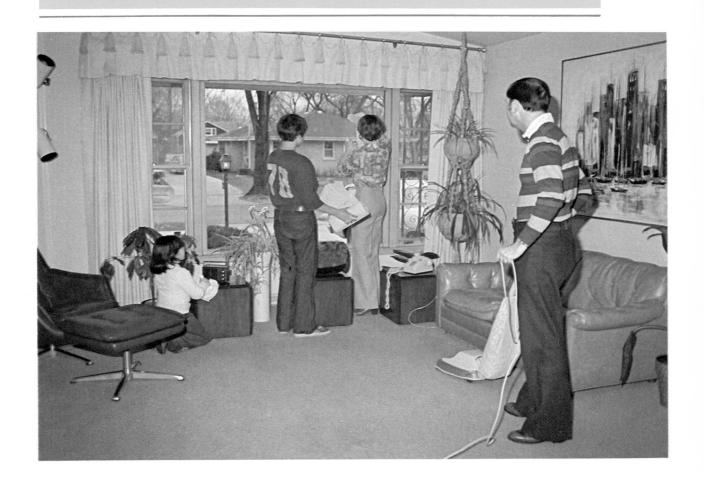

Home is where you live.

Your family lives in a home.

You work at home.

You have good times at home.

35

Home Is Where A Family Lives

A family must have a home.

A family <u>needs</u> a home.

Homes are different.

36

You might live in one of these homes.

What Is A Home For Your Family?

You can make a picture of home.

What will your family need?

Where will people in your family sleep?

How big a home does your family need?

LOOKING AND THINKING

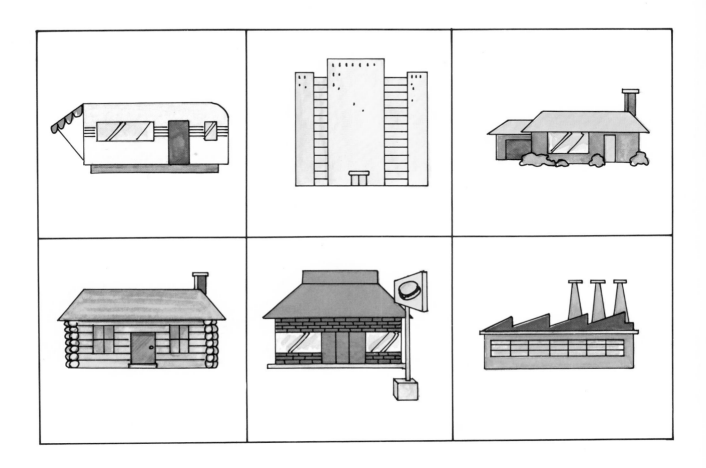

Which ones do you think are homes?

Why?

Which ones are not homes?

Why not?

Families Work At Home

The family is at home.

They are having fun.

What will they have to do soon?

40

It is time to work.

They all help.

They all work.

DIAGRAM
SKILLS

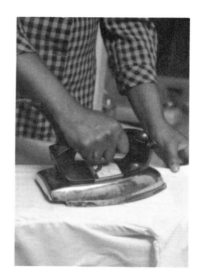

Families work in their homes many days.

What Work Do People In The Family Do?

What work will Father or Mother do?

What work will the children do?

What other work can people

in the family do?

43

Families Can Have Good Times At Home

This family is at home.

They worked today.

How are they having a good time here?

What are they doing?

44

This family is having a good time.

What are they doing?

What does your family do to

have a good time?

How Can Your Family Have Fun At Home?

What can your family do with the ball?

What can you do with the books?

What can you do with the other things?

Does your family have fun at home?

How?

To Talk About And To Do GROUP ACTIVITY

Think of something that needs to be
done at school.

Tell how all the children can help.

Then do what you talked about.

Check What You Know EVALUATION

1. Where does a family live?

2. Who works in the family?

3. How can people in the family help

one another?

Learning By Doing TIME SKILLS

Talk to people who are old.

Find out how they helped at home

long ago.

Make a picture story about them.

The family wants to go to the zoo.

What would you do?

| GENERALIZING | **Checking Ideas** |

1. Why do families need homes?

2. Why is helping one another a help
to all?

3. What kinds of fun can all the
family have?

Rules tell people what to do.

Is there a rule here?

How do rules help you?

Who makes rules?

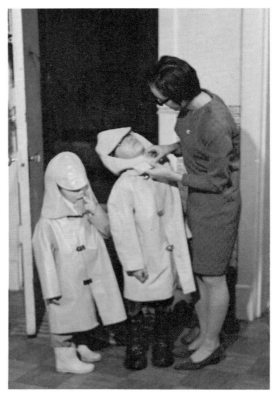

Here Are Family Rules

Rules tell people what to do.

Families make rules.

Rules help people.

How do rules help?

Does your family have rules like these?

What is
the rule here?
How will
it help?

What is
the rule here?
How will
it help?

Why Do We Need Rules?

What rule does he need?

How will it help?

What rule does he need?

How will it help?

52

What rule is needed here?
Why?

What rule is needed here?
Why?

Rules Can Help People

Some rules help people stay well. Some rules help people stay happy. How does a rule help here?

What rule helps here? How will this help people stay well?

This family has a rule.

What could it be?

Does the rule help the family?

Why?

How Can Rules Help At Home?

This family is having a good time.

They know the rules.

Can rules help them to have a good time?

How?

Can rules help you when you play?

How?

Families Make Rules In Different Ways

Mother makes some family rules.

Father makes some family rules.

Some times Mother and Father make rules.

Look at the pictures.

Does your family have these rules?

Who made these rules in your family?

Look first.

Put out lights.

Wash before eating.

Put things away.

Melissa's work
- wash dishes
- make bed
- walk dog

Some times all the people in the family make rules.

Why does your family make rules?

What are rules all the people in your family make?

What Rules Do Families Need?

What rule would
help here?

What rule would
help here?

What other family rules
do you know?

We use rules for many things we do.

Look at the picture.

Which people are using rules?

Why do you think they are using rules?

Which are not using rules?

Why do you think they are not using rules?

To Talk About And To Do

How do rules help with games?

Make up rules for a game for all to play.

Why is it good for all to play?

Check What You Know

1. What are rules?

2. Why do people need rules?

3. What people in the home need rules?

Learning By Doing

List four rules in your family.

Ask for four from your friends.

Are some of the rules the same?

Make a picture to show all the rules.

Show the ones that are the same.

VALUING	**Building Values**

What would you do?

Would a rule help?

What rules would you make?

GENERALIZING	**Checking Ideas**

1. How can rules help people?

2. What rules does your family have?

3. How does your family make rules?

Is there something you want?

Is it something you need?

How can you get things you want or need?

Things You Need And Things You Want

You need many things to live.

You eat.

You need food.

You dress.

You need clothes.

You need some where to live.

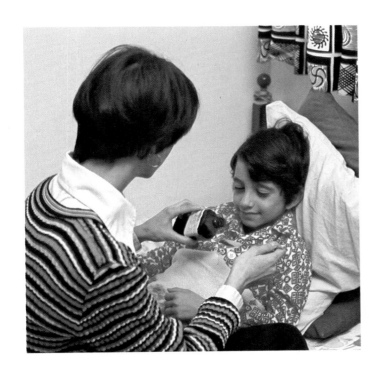

You need other people.

Other people help you.

You need things to live.

You need food, clothes, and

some where to live.

But you want many things, too.

Wants are things you like to have.

But you do not need them to live.

Many children want these things.

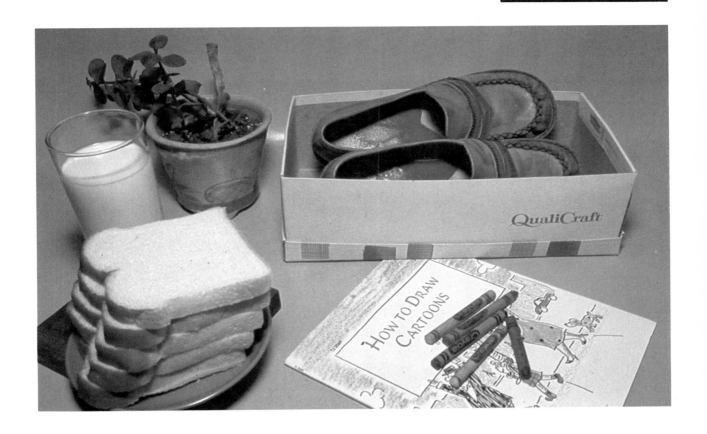

How Are Wants Different From Needs?

There are many things you want.

You do not need these things.

Which things in the picture are wants?

Which things are needs?

Different people have different needs.

Which things do you need?

Which things do the people in the

pictures need?

68

People Work In Many Ways

Some people work making things.

Some people work here.

They work inside.

Others work here.

They work outside.

Some people do things
for others.

They <u>serve</u> them.

Some work with people.

Others work at home.

What Work Do People Do?

What work do you see being done here?

Which people are making things?

Which are serving others?

Which work could you do?

What Money From Work Does

People get money from work.

People get things they need
with their money.

They _buy_ these things.

They buy things
they want with
their money.

How Would You Use Money?

You must buy for your family.

What things would you buy first?

Then what would you buy?

To Talk About And To Do

What kinds of work do people do

for money?

Bring pictures of these kinds of work.

Show the pictures.

Is all the work needed?

Why?

Check What You Know

1. What things do you need?

2. What do we call things we like to have?

3. What two kinds of work do people do?

Learning By Doing

Print Want and Need on paper.

Draw something you want under Want.

Draw something you need under Need.

Building Values

People work for money.

Which work would you do for money?

Why?

Checking Ideas

1. What are three needs you have?

2. What are three wants you have?

3. What are three kinds of work you want to do?

At school you find out about new things.

Who are people who help at school?

How do they help?

What rules do you need at school?

77

You Find Out

New Things At School

You find out about new things at school.

You <u>learn.</u>

You learn about other people.

You learn to play.

You learn to work.

What Do You Learn In School?

What are these children doing?

What do you learn
in school?

What are they
learning?

Many People Help At School

People at school help in different ways.

Some people help you learn.

A <u>teacher</u> helps you learn.

Here are people who help you at school.

Others help you get to school.

CHART
SKILLS

How Do People Help At School?

Who is helping here?

What are they doing?

How do they help you?

What other people help at school?

81

Rules For School

You learn many rules at school.

Some rules help you work with others.

What rule is this?

Some rules tell you what to do in school.

What rule is this?

Some rules help you play with others.

What rules do you see here?

What Are Some School Rules?

What rule do you
see here?
Is this rule needed?
Why?

What rule do you
see here?
Why would this rule
help you at school?
What are rules
at your school?

83

You can see some rules here.

What rules do you see?

Which are rules for home?

Which are rules for school?

Which are rules for home and school?

To Talk About And To Do GROUP ACTIVITY

What are some new things to learn
at school?

Tell the things all of you want to learn.

Tell the things some of you want to learn.

Tell how you will work in different ways
to learn things.

Check What You Know EVALUATION

1. What do children do at school?

2. What are rules for?

3. How do rules help you at school?

Learning By Doing DIAGRAM SKILLS

Make a picture of the inside
of your school.

Show people working in different places.

Building Values

Here are things to learn.

Which one would you learn?

Would you learn more than one?

Why?

Checking Ideas

1. What new things have you learned in school?

2. Who helps at your school?

3. What are rules at your school?

Did you learn to make something to eat?

Is this the way you learned?

How did you learn?

Are there other things you want to learn?

Many Ways To Learn

You go to school to learn.

You learn in many ways.

You learn by things you see
and hear.

You learn from others.

You learn by making things.   You learn by things you do.

What Are Ways You Learn?

What can you learn from this?

What way do you learn?

What other ways can you learn about this?

Places To Learn

This is a <u>place</u> to learn.   This is a place to learn.

There are other places to learn, too.

Here is one you will like.

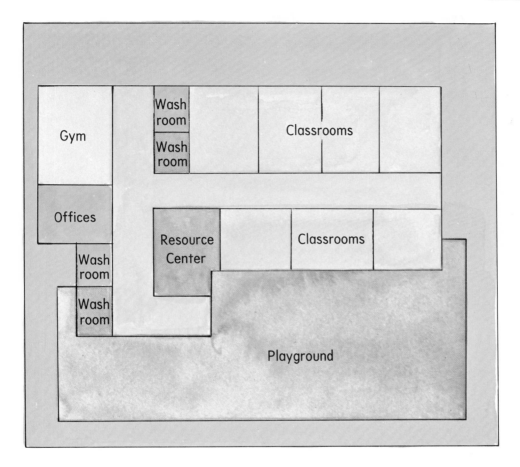

MAP
SKILLS

Where Do You Work At School?

You can see places where you learn.

What places do you see?

What do you learn?

Where do you learn in your school?

91

You can learn many things.

There are many ways to learn.

What ways to learn do you see

in this picture?

Who is not learning?

To Talk About And To Do   GROUP ACTIVITY

Talk about places where you learn.

How do others help you learn?

Do something to help others learn.

Check What You Know   EVALUATION

1. What do you do at school?

2. Who helps you learn?

3. What is one other place people from school may go to learn?

4. What are two things you do that help you learn?

Learning By Doing   MAP SKILLS

Make a picture showing places at your school where you learn.

Show a name for each place.

Building Values

How would you learn about a farm?

Is there just one way to learn?

Would you like to learn in more ways?

Why?

GENERALIZING **Checking Ideas**

1. Where are places you learn?

2. Who helps you learn?

3. What are different ways to learn?

94

This is a picture of the <u>earth.</u>

It is the place where you and
other people live.

What can you tell about the earth
from what you see?

GLOBE
SKILLS

A Globe Shows The Earth

The earth is like a ball.

A <u>globe</u> is a ball.

A globe shows all the earth.

The earth has <u>land</u>.

You live on land.

This globe shows the land in brown.

This globe shows the water in blue.

This globe shows what the land
and water are named.

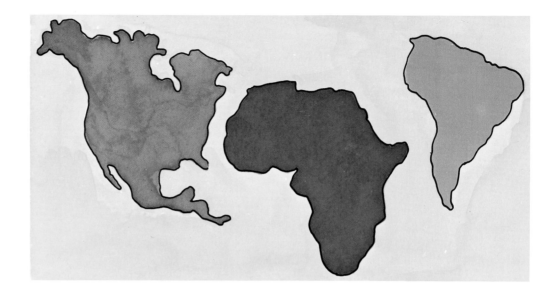

What Do You See On A Globe?

Find the places in the picture
on a globe.

Many of you live in one
of the places.

It is called North America.

What are the names of the other
two places you found?

A Map Shows Some Of The Earth

A <u>map</u> can show places on earth.

A map can show one place.

This is a picture of a place.

This is a map of the same place.

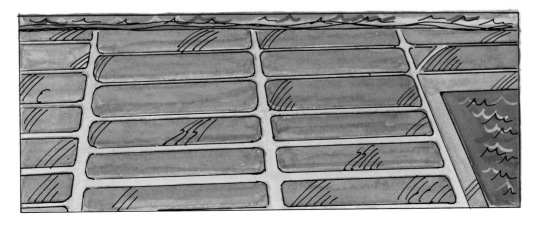

MAP SKILLS

A map shows where things are.

A map may show many things about
a place on the earth.

How Can A Map Help You?

You live in House A.

You are going to House B and House C.

Then you are going to school.

Tell how you go to school.

You want to go to the store from your house.

Tell how you would go.

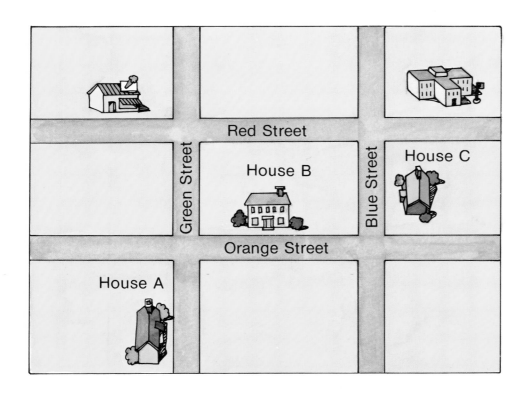

MAP SKILLS

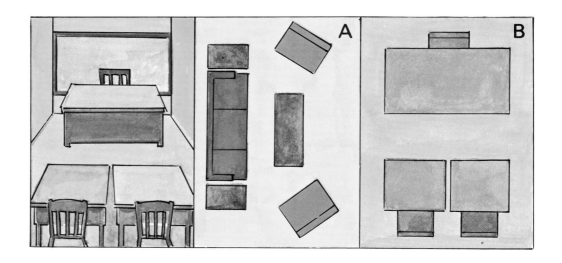

Here is a picture of a place at school.

One of the maps shows the same place.

Does Map A or Map B show the place
in the picture?

What things do you see in the map and
in the picture?

What things do you see in the picture
and not on the map?

What maps can you make to help you?

102

Families In Many Places

Families live in many places on the earth.

The places may be hot or cold.

They may be on land or water.

There are many ways the places may be different.

The families may live in different ways.

They may live in ways that are the same, too.

**How Are Homes Different
In Different Places?**

Which home is in a place that is hot?

Which home is in a place where water comes on the land?

What things about your home show something about the place where you live?

104

To Talk About And To Do GROUP ACTIVITY

Talk about the things all families do.

Tell how living where it is hot is different

from living where it is cold.

Bring pictures to show how people live

in different places.

Put the pictures up for all to see.

Check What You Know EVALUATION

1. What does the globe show?

2. Is water on the globe blue or brown?

3. What does a map show?

4. Where do families live on the earth?

Learning By Doing MAP SKILLS

Find a picture of a place.

Make a map of it.

You are going to live in a new place.

Which of the things you see here can help

you find out about your new home?

How could they help you?

| GENERALIZING | **Checking Ideas** |

1. What things does a globe show?

2. How are maps and globes the same?
   How are they different?

3. What may homes show about the place
   where people live?

A <u>country</u> is a place.

A country is people.

What is your country?

What can you do for your country?

107

Days For The Country

There are days people remember.

There are days for the country.

This is the birthday of the country.

It is the 4th of July.

108

George Washington

(1732-1799)

George Washington liked to work on his farm.

The people of the country needed him.

He went to help the country.

The people liked what he did.

The people made him President.

The country has a day to remember him.

What work did George Washington like?

Why did he go away from his work?

How Do People Remember Days For The Country?

This is a day to remember.

It is a day to give thanks.

How does your family remember this day?

People Of Your Country

Many people have helped this country.

People now help this country, too.

All the people can help.

They help in different ways.

This is one way to help.

This is a rule.

People use the rule.

This helps the country, too.

How Do People Help The Country?

People work and play.

They use rules and learn.

They help other people.

This helps make a good country.

How are these people helping the country?

How do people you know help?

113

There Are Ways For You To Help Your Country

You can help your country in many ways.

You can learn.   You can help.

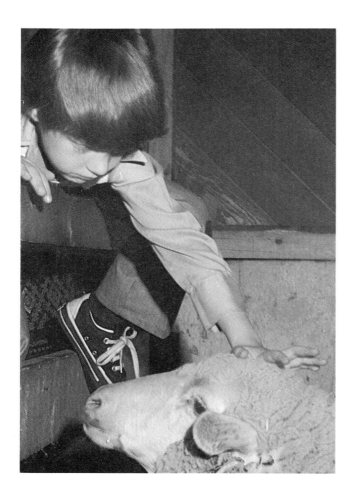

114

What Can You Do For Your Country?

How do these people show they remember their country?

What can you do here?

What can you do here?

You can do some things for your

country now.

You can do some when you are older.

You can do some things now and when

you are older.

Tell which pictures show how you can help.

116

To Talk About And To Do GROUP ACTIVITY

Talk about a day for people to remember.

Tell what you do to remember the day.

Do some things to remember the day.

Check What You Know EVALUATION

1. What day is the country's birthday?

2. What is the day people give thanks?

3. How do people help the country?

4. What can you do at school to help

the country?

5. Who can help the country?

Learning By Doing RESOURCE SKILLS

Some people helped the country.

We remember them.

Find out about some one who helped.

Tell the other children about him or her.

117

Building Values

There are different ways to help.

What would you do here?

Checking Ideas

1. What do we do on days to remember
for the country?

2. What kinds of things do people do
to help the country?

3. What do you do to help your country?

VOCABULARY

The suggested reading level of this book is first grade. The total number of different words in this book, excluding social studies concept words and proper nouns, is 159. The words listed below are first grade words except for the eleven words shown in italics. The italicized words are above level.

All words are listed alphabetically. The number indicates the page on which the word first appears.

ago 47
another 47
as 12

baby 12
back 28
be(ing) 71
better 33
boy 5
bring 17
brown 97

children 17
cold 102
could 55

day 17
done 47
dress 64

farm 94
find 47
first 31
food 64
four 31

game(s) 61
girl 5
gone 25

had 22
happy 11
hear 30

her 22
hot 103
how 9

if 17
inside 69

just 11

kind(s) 76

list 61
live 35
long 28

many 22
money 72
more 17
must 36

name 93

old 9
older 17
or 5
other 5
outside 69

picture 12
President 109

same 16
school 14

sleep 38
sing 30
stay 34
store 101
story 47

talk 17
tell 17
their 42
them 8
there 26
these 16
thing(s) 19
think 11
three 20
time(s) 11
today 44

under 75

very 10

water 97
way(s) 8
well 54
were 10
when 12
where 35
which 12
why 17
would 18

zoo 48

SOCIAL STUDIES CONCEPT WORDS

buy 73	family 20	people 15
changed 10	globe 96	place 90
clothes 64	land 97	remember 28
country 107	learn 78	rules 49
different 8	map 99	serve 70
earth 95	needs 36	teacher 80

ACKNOWLEDGMENTS

Artists: Bill Anderson
Sally Manion

Photographer: Joe Speno

Our thanks to the following for permission to reproduce the photographs that appear on the pages indicated.

Chicago Police Department, 112
Columbia Records, 30
Environmental Protection Agency, Berkey K + L Custom Service, 111
Harrington, Richard, 103 (right)
Lambert, Harold M., 29, 99 (left)
Photography Unlimited, 114 (left)
Rohn Engh, 23, 69 (bottom)
Schirmer, Mathilda, 104 (left)